HUMOR
IN THE
SALT MINES

HUMOR
IN THE
SALT MINES

A Master Lawyer's Guide
to Associate Success

ASA ROUNTREE
Edited by Lorna G. Schofield

Cover by Elmarie Jara /ABA Publishing.
Text design, editing, and typesetting by Rodelinde Albrecht.
Chapter opening art by Christopher J. Hammond.

The materials contained herein represent the opinions and views of the authors and/or the editors, and should not be construed to be the views or opinions of the law firms or companies with whom such persons are in partnership with, associated with, or employed by, nor of the Section of Litigation or First Chair Press, unless adopted pursuant to the bylaws of the Association.

Nothing contained in this book is to be considered as the rendering of legal advice for specific cases, and readers are responsible for obtaining such advice from their own legal counsel. This book is intended for educational and informational purposes only.

Printed in the United States of America

17 16 15 14 13   5 4 3

Library of Congress Cataloging-in-Publication Data on File

ISBN 978-1-62722-173-3

Discounts are available for books ordered in bulk. Special consideration is given to state bars, CLE programs, and other bar-related organizations. Inquire at Book Publishing, ABA Publishing, American Bar Association, 321 North Clark Street, Chicago, Illinois 60654-7598.

www.ShopABA.org

Contents

Foreword

Asa Rountree was a true Renaissance gentleman, in the very best sense of those words. His interests and talents were enormously broad. He was a dedicated father and husband. He loved to ski and play tennis. He was an artist and a prolific writer, and of course a great lawyer, and he brought passion, boundless energy, and garrulous good cheer to all of his work. He was a member of the American College of Trial Lawyers and an early founder of the Litigation Section of the American Bar Association.

Asa was a proud son of the South. He was born in Birmingham, Alabama, and graduated from the University of Alabama before graduating magna cum laude from Harvard Law School. He served in the Army in both the Second World War and the Korean War where he saw combat first as a rifle platoon leader and then as assistant battalion operations officer. He began the practice of law in Birmingham in 1954 with the distinguished law firm of Cabaniss & Johnson, where he became a partner. He was such an accomplished trial lawyer that Samuel Gates, the senior litigation partner at what was then Debevoise, Plimpton, Lyons & Gates, in New York City, recruited Asa in 1962 to join the litigation department at Debevoise where he again promptly became a partner.

Asa's clients loved him. Among those clients, he counted giants in the worlds of finance, government, accounting, publishing, and sports, to name a few. Asa would frown on naming any specific clients because, as he once explained, "public record is not necessarily public knowledge, and often clients do not like to have it bruited about that they are being sued. Nor does a client like a lawyer bragging about his representation of the client."

Asa represented his clients with tireless energy. His hours were legendary. He had a famous cot in his office, and he tried to reduce the amount of sleep that he really needed. He thought that if he could get along on less sleep, he could pack more into the day. One time Asa, as a leader of the Section of Litigation, attended the Litigation Section meeting in Hawaii. He traveled out one day, attended the meeting the next day and then headed back to New York to return to client business. He had tremendous drive, a restless desire to accomplish all that he could in the very limited time that was available, and so he tried to stretch the day and crowd all that he could into that limited time.

Asa was a founding member of the Litigation Section and served in numerous leadership positions, including chair of the section from 1980 through 1981. In his final column as chair, Asa reflected on the work of the Section and described its activities as "acting responsibly and energetically to assure that the litigation process remains responsive to the needs of society." He concluded "without equivocation that the trial bar is alive and well and is as independent and contentious as ever. As long as that be so, the Republic need not fear for its freedom."

These are simply some of the objective facts of Asa's practice of law. Even more important than the objective facts is the spirit with which Asa practiced law. Asa was always a gentleman. He was gracious and straightforward. He practiced civility in the days before civility became a compliment. He avoided Rambo tactics without sacrificing the best interests of his clients.

You could trust Asa's word. In negotiations, if he said something was unacceptable, you knew he would not agree to it. It was time to move on to something else. He was not prone to self-aggrandizement, bombast, or boasting. He had credibility because judges and adversaries knew that they could trust his word. If he said he would do something, he would do it.

But this graciousness did not mean that Asa would compromise his client's interests. He was tough when he had to be, even if that toughness was expressed in a soft voice and a Southern accent.

Asa lived and preached professionalism. In 1975, he wrote a legendary memo (which he later updated) to associates who worked with him. That memo is the centerpiece of this book. It details many of the things associates should do in representing clients zealously and professionally. What is so striking about the memo is its emphasis on unflinching dedication to the client's interests, even though the work may be difficult and involve personal hardship. The memo is also characterized by the refreshing writing and humor that we learned to love and expect from Asa. At one point, Asa defines a professional as "one who professes vows to a calling requiring specialized knowledge and often long and intensive academic preparation." With characteristic humor, Asa also provides an alternative definition of a professional: "a person who does a good job even when he doesn't feel like it."

The memo also reflects the personal sacrifices Asa was prepared to make in order to get the work done and safeguard the personal lives of the associates. With leadership comes even greater responsibility, and perhaps even greater work. At one point, Asa talks to associates about the possibility of night and weekend work: "If taking an assignment or meeting a deadline means that you will have to cancel personal plans that are meaningful to you — or, more important, are meaningful to a meaningful person, whether spouse, child, or otherwise — under no circumstances are you to cancel those plans without first consulting with me. There may be alternatives. Why, I may even do the work myself."

One of the concluding thoughts in the memo is the following advice: "[L]ife is a broader tapestry than the practice of the law. There is a big, wide, wonderful world out there. Don't miss it." That surely is the Renaissance gentleman speaking.

Asa was a gentleman with everyone with whom he worked. He once commented that when he came to Debevoise in the early 1960s, a stenographer in the steno pool kept asking to be assigned to Asa, so Asa asked her why that was so, and she said "you're the only lawyer who says thank you." Asa's booming laugh and infectious smile were joys for those who worked with him.

Here is how one of Asa's former partners at Debevoise aptly described him: "Most important of all, it is fun working with Asa. Whether an issue is legal or ethical, business or personal, sticky or simple, he makes it fun. And one comes away comfortable with the analysis and the conclusion. There is a validity to Asa's advice that is rooted not only in a sound analytical approach or a logical arrangement of pros and cons — many lawyers can fashion reasons for a position — but in that quality of character that knows what is just, fair, and honorable, that internal gyroscope we call integrity."

Asa was a constant advocate for greater training and organization within Debevoise, and in the litigation department in particular. He attempted to attract small-case litigation to provide training opportunities for young lawyers, and he took mentoring very seriously. He peppered his colleagues with numerous memos on how the firm and the litigation department could be improved. And if he could not convince others within the firm to follow his suggestions, he would at least implement his suggestions for himself and those who worked with him. Those memos are a gift to those who have followed him.

Throughout his tenure, Asa advanced his ideas with persistence but with genial good cheer and a thorough appreciation of the firm's culture. As he once put it, "My memoranda reflect an abiding interest in the firm's professionalism, in the high quality of the firm's work, and in the collegiality and informality of the firm's culture, a culture that made Debevoise a wonderful place in which to spend most of my professional career." Asa was being too modest; he failed to point out the fact that Debevoise was the place it was, in no small part due to the role that Asa played in making it so. He was one of the anchors of the litigation department, which became an ever-increasing part of the firm. He was responsible for bringing major clients to the firm and was one of the forces that helped to preserve the vigor and vitality of the firm while other firms with storied pedigrees did not survive.

When Asa retired from Debevoise in 1991, he returned to practice law in Birmingham and became a shareholder in the firm of Maynard, Cooper & Gale, where Lee Cooper, another former chair of the Litigation Section and a former president of the American Bar Association, was a senior partner. Lee Cooper has said that Asa's return to the firm was particularly important because of the role Asa played in sharing his wisdom with younger lawyers and mentoring them.

Asa helped to shape generations of lawyers through his example and his teaching. Each of us who was privileged to work with Asa has been influenced by him and carries on what he taught. The great joy of the memos collected in this volume is that they help to spread that wisdom.

Judge John G. Koeltl

Since 1994, Judge Koeltl has been a judge in the United States District Court for the Southern District of New York. Before that, he was a partner at Debevoise & Plimpton LLP. He practiced law with Asa Rountree at Debevoise from 1975 until Asa's retirement in 1991.

Preface

I knew Asa as my neighbor in the big corner office just down the hall when I was a new, but fairly senior, associate at Debevoise & Plimpton. Although we never worked together, he was one of my first friends at the firm. He stopped in occasionally to say hello. I visited his office from time to time to ask questions. Later, long after he had retired and left New York for Alabama and I was myself a seasoned partner, I followed in his footsteps and was elected Chair of the American Bar Association Litigation Section. The shared experience rekindled our friendship, which I enjoyed the last several years of his life. I feel honored that he was a friend, and admire to this day his ability to have fun while practicing law as intensely and professionally as could be done.

Once he showed me a brief he was about to submit and asked for my comments. Although reluctant to be critical, I did tell him I did not care for one very clever (too clever) phrase in the brief. He thought about it, and then said that he advised his young colleagues that, if there is one word or phrase that they especially love in a brief, they should take it out. It draws attention to itself and away from the argument. The writing, he said, should be transparent. He said that he had failed to take his own advice and would take out the offending phrase.

That advice was in the spirit of the memorandum that is the central work in this book. We passed the memo around at the firm from generation to generation. After Asa died, his wife, Helen Hill Rountree, and I wanted to find a way to share it with a broader audience. Helen (as interesting a partner as you might expect of Asa) first brought forward the idea of publishing the memo, with proceeds from its sale to fund pro bono work by the Litigation Section to honor Asa.

To Helen, the memo is not only an invaluable guide for how to be a fine lawyer, but also a wise and thoughtful primer on how to be a worthy practitioner of any profession. Helen deserves the credit for supplying several other of Asa's writings included here, as well as providing the portrait of Asa shown on the back cover.

Thanks also to my judicial assistant, Barton Lewis, for his invaluable help in readying the book for production.

Asa's advice is timeless and true, but also hints at the pleasure that can be had in aiming to practice law at the highest level.

Judge Lorna G. Schofield

CHAPTER ONE

Guidelines for Work
Being Done under My Supervision

INTRODUCTION

Sometimes a partner fails properly to inform an associate of what is expected. This memorandum is an attempt to minimize that risk when an associate is working with me. It speaks for me and for me alone. Its intent is to supplement the instructions that have been given to you by others for whom you may be working. In the event of inconsistency, their instructions govern, of course.

GENERAL EXPECTANCY

Your work should be viewed in the light of what our clients expect. They expect superb work, produced on time and at reasonable cost, and performed and delivered in a professional manner.

PROFESSIONALISM

We are professionals, you and I. A professional is one who "professes" vows to "a calling requiring specialized knowledge and often long and intensive academic preparation."* Sometimes there is tension between a lawyer's professional obligation of "zealous representation" and other professional obligations. Sometimes there is tension between professional obligations and other obligations, such as obligation to family or self, or to moral principle, or to the community, or to the economic success of the law firm. When that tension occurs, it has to be resolved, and in a manner that satisfies *all* of a lawyer's obligations. Often, that is not easy.

CLIENT RELATIONSHIPS

This is no place to explore the complexities of client relationships. I will say only this: The word client comes from the Latin *cliens*, *clientis* (dependent), akin to *clinare* (to lean). That is to say, your client is a per-

---

* Another definition of a professional is "a person who does a good job even when he doesn't feel like it." This reminds me of Winston Churchill, who once said, "Most of the work of the world is done by people who don't feel very well."

4

son who leans upon you in the sense that he* depends on you and looks to you for protection. This means, among other things, that you must not only competently handle your client's case, but you must also inspire confidence in yourself. Usually, a client does not need to be told time and again that he has a problem. He knows he has a problem. That's why he came to you. He's looking to you to solve the problem.

You have to be on your client's side, and he has to feel that you are on his side. If for some reason you cannot really be on your client's side—and that sometimes happens—you should withdraw from representation. Don't preach to the client, don't tell him he's greedy or rapacious, don't urge him to repent of his sins and seek salvation. Just withdraw.

CONFIDENTIALITY

Quite apart from the attorney–client privilege, which I address later, it is essential to maintain confidentiality with respect to client affairs. This requires con-

* For convenience herein, masculine personal pronouns are used in their impersonal sense. Believe me, I am not insensitive to gender-neutral language. I continue to experiment with it, as you will see. But it sure is a strain on style.

stant vigilance, often in ways that may not spring readily to mind. For example:

1. Confidential client information is not to be revealed to a spouse or next best friend, either or both.
2. On an airline or at a cocktail party or in a restaurant or any other place where people are gathered together, you must use the utmost discretion in discussing client matters. It is beyond belief how much information can be picked up in a restaurant. At restaurants, some folks become so intent on their own conversation that they forget big ears are at nearby tables.
3. You must be careful in elevators. This often re- quires self-discipline because if, while waiting for an elevator you are involved in a discussion about a legal matter, your tendency, particularly if you are making a devastating point, may be to con- tinue the discussion in the elevator.* You must

* Recently, I was at the back of a crowded elevator in our building. At the front of the elevator two young people (whom I did not recognize) were talking about a legal problem. I said in a voice distinct enough for most people in the elevator to look at me with surprise, "If you are from Debevoise [my firm], please don't talk business in the elevator." Those two young people kept talking. Then I repeated myself in a voice loud enough for God himself to hear, "If you are from Debevoise, please don't talk business in the elevator." The two young people turned and glared at me. "We are *not* from Debevoise," they said.

resist this impulse and hold your tongue until you are in a private place.

Even when our representation of a client is a matter of public record, you must be careful about what, if anything, you say about that representation. Public record is not necessarily public knowledge, and often clients do not like to have it bruited about that they are being sued. Nor does a client like a lawyer bragging about his representation of the client.

When you are discussing legal matters on your speakerphone, you should close your door. There are three reasons:

1. lots of strangers walk the halls and can overhear confidential information,
2. the person on the other end of the phone might be perturbed to have his remarks heard all the way down the hall, particularly if he, like me, is prone to earthy language, and
3. the speakerphone is often disturbing to your next-door neighbors.

ASSUMPTION OF RESPONSIBILITY

You should assume *full* responsibility for your assignment. I mean by this that you should consider all the problems of the assignment to be *your* problems. Your responsibility runs directly to the client, who provides your sustenance as well as mine.

You should approach an assignment as if you were a sole practitioner, with no one to review or criticize or correct your work, and with final and irredeemable responsibility for the client's cause. You should be skeptical, inquisitive, imaginative, energetic, and thorough. You should not be impressed by my analysis of the issues or my views about their probable resolution. You should assume that I am over the hill and am no longer capable of discerning the issues, much less analyzing or resolving them. You should look for the questions I should have asked but did not. On an administrative level, you should not assume that I have reserved a conference room, ordered coffee or lunch, called for a court reporter, arranged for transportation, or, when we are traveling together, that I have money or even a subway token. In short, do not rely on me; I am relying on you.

When you send me written material, make sure that it gets to my attention when it ought to get to my attention. Communicating in the usual way may not do the job. The information flow is so great that even important documents may not leap to my attention. If I need to see material immediately, let my secretary or me know that it's on the way or bring it yourself. In the latter event, if I am out of my office, place the material, not on my messy desk, but on my chair. I may not know where I'm going, but I always look where I sit.

DEADLINES

There are two types of deadlines, the internally imposed deadline and the externally imposed deadline. You should be sensitive to both.

Internal Deadlines

When I give you an assignment, I will generally give you a deadline. If I do not, you should ask for one. In some instances, you will be asked to set your own deadline. In any event, the deadline should be met. You should not take a relaxed view of an internal deadline just because it seems comfortably in advance of the external deadline to which the assignment may relate. After all, your work may have to be done over. It has happened before. I need sufficient leeway for that eventuality.

External Deadlines

In transactional matters, external deadlines are set by the client or by the dynamics of the particular transaction. Sometimes the deal is dead if the deadline is not met. That is what is meant by the word *deadline*. In litigation, external deadlines are set by law, by rule of court, by order of court, or by stipulation with an adversary. Those deadlines, too, are for real. In some instances, they are jurisdictional in nature; in others, they relate to the Statute of Limitations. When the axe of the Statute has fallen, it has fallen forever. You cannot sew the head back on the body.

Extensions of Time

Extensions of time can often be obtained, either by negotiation with your adversary or by application to the court,* but you should *never* assume that an extension can in fact be obtained. You must schedule your work and your request for an extension so that if the request is denied, you have time to complete the job. In this regard, follow my precept, not my occasional example. I may seem relaxed about obtaining an extension of time. If so, it is because I know my adversary very well, or know precisely what I can expect from a particular judge. But I remain nervous until I actually have the extension.

Conflicting Responsibilities

Our associates have primary responsibility for managing their own workload. In exercising that responsibility, you must realistically evaluate your work situation when responding to requests from other partners to take on additional work. When you are faced with a deadline which, if it is to be met, means that you will miss a deadline for another partner, you must serve as an honest broker in resolving the conflict. You must take the initia-

* Indeed, what I do best in the practice of law is obtain extensions of time.

tive of going to the partners involved, and you must do so sufficiently in advance of the deadlines so that appropriate adjustments can be made.* I tend toward apoplexy if an associate, on the last day, tells me for the first time that my job has not been completed because of an intervening crisis that took place five days earlier.

Night and Weekend Work

Sometimes, in order to meet a deadline, it is necessary to work nights and weekends. If taking an assignment or meeting a deadline means that you will have to cancel personal plans that are meaningful to you—or, more important, are meaningful to a meaningful person, whether spouse, child, or otherwise— under no circumstances are you to cancel those plans without first consulting with me. There may be alternatives. Why, I might even do the work myself. The same may be true of other partners as well.

---

* This is not to say that you yourself have no responsibility for giving priorities to the jobs you have. On the contrary, you have great responsibility. But in setting priorities you should be warned that it is the job that counts, not what you perceive to be the status of the partners involved.

NATURE OF WORK PRODUCT

Unless I have given explicit instructions to the contrary (which I sometimes do when speed is more important than style or even thoroughness), I shall assume that any writing you prepare and deliver to me represents the *very best* you can do. Labeling the writing as a draft is not a disclaimer. A poorly executed written assignment will live much longer and be more damning than the faint memory of your declining a work assignment because of other pressing work matters.

LEGAL RESEARCH

Many young lawyers dislike research. This is regrettable. Unless one has decided to commit oneself to a very narrow area of the law, extensive research of a diversity of problems over a long period of time is valuable to a mastery of the learning, thinking, and analyzing processes of the law.

Your research should be thorough and up to date. By *thorough*, I do not mean that you should cite every case decided since 1686 standing for the proposition that, generally, there must be a meeting of the minds before a contract comes into being. Judiciousness and common sense are always in order. Each research problem has its own requirements. Your responsibility is to be sure that the particular requirements of the particular job are met.

Attached as Appendix 1 is a research checklist I contrived for my own use many years ago. It may be helpful, but it is old, like me, and, like me, should be viewed very skeptically.

CITATIONS AND QUOTATIONS

When you submit a writing that includes legal citations, whether the writing be a draft or a final product, whether it be a memorandum or a brief or a letter opinion, all the citations should have been checked in all respects (names, numbers, abbreviations, form, punctuation, subsequent history, and so on). All cases should have been checked to confirm that they are still good law, and all quotations should have been proofed. Short quotations can be checked by eye. Long quotations should be proofed with someone else.* If, for any reason, the foregoing has

---

* When I practiced law in Birmingham, Alabama, every brief filed by my firm was actually proofed by two lawyers, at least one of whom was a partner. (Incidentally, *this* memorandum has *not* been proofed. At least, that's my cover story, which you should not ever use.)

not been done, a caveat to that effect should be emblazoned on the first page of the writing. The word *draft* is not a sufficient caveat.

When you cite a case, it means to me that you have actually read the case; that it stands for the proposition for which it is cited; that you have made the best use of it for our purposes; and that, unless you have raised a red flag for me, the case contains neither facts or holdings nor *dicta* that are harmful to our cause. Too often, a case properly cited for a general proposition will be found, when I read it (as I will), to contain harmful material.* Another error is to take a powerful case in our favor and merely cite it. This won't do. Favorable authority is too often too scarce. When you have a good case, work with it. Linger over it. Massage it. Manipulate it. Make it do a soft-shoe dance.

STYLE OF WRITING

One learns to write only by writing. Moreover, each person develops his own individual style of writing, so that I can say nothing helpful about style ex-

* An effective ploy in a reply brief is to take the enemy's cases and turn them back against him. In this regard, one of the first things to do upon receipt of an opposing brief is to take it to the library and check out the cases cited therein.

cept to urge you to experiment with different styles. I do make the observation—which ought not to be necessary—that different writings have different purposes and call for different styles. A law review article, for example, is generally designed to promote some bias of the author or to display his erudition. The purpose of a memorandum of law is to compile the law, analyze the law, assess different strategies, raise storm warnings, and the like. The purpose of a brief is to persuade.

In a brief, you should try for brevity and forcefulness. Long quotations, like long sentences, are generally to be avoided. Quoted material is often more effective if it can be worked smoothly into the text. In a memorandum, on the other hand, particularly if it is a preliminary memorandum, it may be desirable to include longer quotations. These can later be cut down or worked into the text.

Attached as Appendix 2 is a memorandum entitled *Brief Writing and Kindred Matters*.

KEEPING EACH OTHER INFORMED

I should keep you informed. You should keep me informed. If the one of us is to do better than the other of us, let the one be you. Incoming correspondence should be routed or copied by the one of us to the other of us. The same is to be done with outgoing correspondence. If you do not keep me informed, I shall complain. If I do not keep you informed, you should complain.

WORK HABITS

I am not sure whether we have a "normal" workday around here or, if so, exactly what it is. Personally, I am more or less indifferent to what your usual work day is, but if it substantially departs from whatever norm we have, I would like to know about it so that I may know your usual availability.*

My own work habits are somewhat idiosyncratic. When needed, of course, I, like all lawyers, am available to clients and other lawyers twenty-

---

* Back in 1973, being always noted for my liberalism, I went whooping and hollering aboard the feminist bandwagon. For one thing, I recommended the adoption of a "gliding" work day, so as to be sensitive to individual needs, particularly the needs of lawyers and staff with young children. Also, I urged that secretaries not be required, requested, or even permitted to serve coffee in conference rooms. That was a new thought in those days.

four hours a day, seven days a week.* Otherwise, except when I am hung over, I am always available (at home or in the office) by 6:00 A.M., earlier in the spring and summer.** I generally get in the office early (somewhere between 6:30 A.M. and 8:30 A.M.), and I try to leave between 5:30 P.M. and 6:00 P.M. unless I am working at night.

FILES

I have created my own decimal system for the indexing of files and documents in a complex case. This is known as the Rountree Decimal System, which bears the same relationship to the Dewey Decimal System that a state-of-the-art computer bears to an abacus. However, I attach as Appendix 3 a skeletal outline of the Rountree Decimal System. Its charm is in its infinite flexibility.

---

* I do not, however, take joy in being called from a gin mill at 3:00 A.M. to be told that you will be in the office ten minutes late that morning.
** When the sun comes up, I come up. Phylogenetically, man is a creature of the day. He is a diurnal predator, not a nocturnal scavenger. When the sun goes down, the nature of man is to seek the safety of the tree or the cave. To do otherwise is to pervert the nature of man. Therein lies the tragedy of the species. Anthropologists have definitively established that the misfortunes of man commenced only when he began to utilize artificial light. It made him cantankerous. That is the true meaning of the Promethean story.

GENERAL AVAILABILITY

If you are not immediately reachable, even for a short period of time, you should ensure that if a court, a client, or I attempt to contact you, we will be told how to reach you immediately if necessary, and when you otherwise can be reached or will respond.

On their face, these instructions may seem unduly intrusive. Let me try to explain: When someone who relies on you as a professional urgently needs to get in touch with you, it is not very helpful to be told "She/he is away from her/his desk." We know that. Otherwise, you would have answered your phone or otherwise responded. What the caller needs to know is *when* you will be available. Once, when I was in the Dallas Airport on my way back to New York, with my plane leaving in ten minutes, it was important for me to reach one of our lawyers in New York. I called. He and his secretary were "away from their desks." The receptionist did not know where they were. Would the lawyer return in ten minutes? In one hour? The receptionist did not know. My urgency was such that, if the lawyer would be available within an hour, I was willing to miss my flight in order to talk with him. What did I do? I really don't remember.

EFFICIENCY

Efficiency is measured by cost, to the extent that cost itself is realistically measured. You should be cost conscious but without diluting the quality of your work. Lawyers' fees are high. We are paid by clients who believe that lawyers are well educated, extremely bright, and highly motivated, and are experienced in the areas in which they practice, or, at least, are under the supervision of experienced lawyers.

In doing your work, you should always consider what procedures and personnel are best suited to the particular task. You should consider whether the task is done better by you or by another lawyer, or by your assistant, by a paralegal, or by the library. Your job is lawyering. Generally speaking, any job that can be done by a nonlawyer is better done by that person than by you. *But this is not always so.* It may be more efficient for you to walk to a copy machine than to unleash staff procedures. Certainly, you should not consider it beneath your dignity to do so. When the occasion demands, I do my own copying, collating, and cite checking, often in the early hours of the morning.

Also, if it takes you two hours at the rate of $200 an hour to do a job, and it takes a legal assistant six hours at the rate of $100 an hour to do the same job, it is more efficient for the client (if not for the profitability of the firm) for you yourself to do the job.

You should also give attention to disbursements. Clients are doing so. I shall do so. In this regard, you should consider such things as how many copies of a document you really need, whether overtime secretarial help is really necessary, whether communications really need to be sent by overnight courier, and how much all these things cost.

In short, when you spend time or money, think about it. But also and always, think quality.

TIME SHEETS

Some folks grumble that I have a "thing" about the prompt submission of time sheets. Well, having been in charge of the firm's finances on two occasions, I confess to the charge.* Although most lawyers are very conscientious about submitting their time, a few

---

* I do not, however, go to the extent of Stanley J. Kumble, the founder of Finley Kumble. Speaking of him, the *New York Times* (September 7, 1990, p. B6) said, among other things: "He also admits to occasional compulsiveness. Once he walked into a partner's office, found him on the floor writhing in pain, and could think of only one thing to say to him: 'Howard, are your time sheets in?'"

are not. The few cost the rest of us money. Since we are professionals, none of us practices law for money. Still, money is very useful when it comes to paying the rent, to say nothing of partner distributions and associate salaries.*

Moreover, it has been my observation and experience that although it is not always true, it is often true that a lawyer who is consistently deficient in the prompt submission of time sheets is deficient in other ways as well (although such deficiencies may not surface for a very long time).

It is essential that timekeeping be accurate. An associate should not adjust his time records according to his own assessment of whether he is working efficiently or inefficiently. That is to say, he should not report less time than he actually spent on the job because he thinks he has spent too much time. Usually, he is wrong in that assessment. In any event, it is the partner's responsibility to make that assessment.

---

* Over the years, I have heard a number of lawyers, partners and associates alike, complain that they are being harassed and treated like clockpunchers when they are admonished to submit their time sheets in prompt fashion. But time sheets are the source of our bills, and our bills are the source of our revenues, and our revenues are the source of our compensation. I give you my word, in 37 years of practice, I have never heard a partner or an associate complain about the prompt payment of his compensation.

And under no circumstances should an associate spend less time on a job than has to be spent to get the job properly done. If more time is spent than can be billed, so be it. It is an event not to be cherished, but it happeneth to all of us.

ATTORNEY–CLIENT PRIVILEGE AND WORK PRODUCT DOCTRINE

You should always keep in mind the protection of the attorney–client privilege and work product doctrine. You should establish, whenever appropriate, procedures to protect that protection.

A matter often overlooked is that the client should be made to understand the *limits* of the attorney–client privilege. Some laymen think that *anything* they tell a lawyer is protected. That is not so. For example, if information is given to a lawyer, not for the purpose of obtaining legal advice, but to further a tort or crime, it is *not* protected. Nor can a lawyer knowingly condone perjury or fraud on a court. Moreover, information given to a lawyer in the presence of third persons, or disclosed to third persons, may not have or may lose the protection of the privilege. If advice-of-counsel is raised as a defense, the privilege is usually held to be waived.

In the course of protecting the privilege and your work product, you should be very careful about your own note taking. Unless you have a more reliable memory than most people, you will have to take notes. But in doing so, you should always bear in mind the possibility that those notes will be subpoenaed. Even if you believe the notes are privileged, the privilege may be lost or waived. So you should be circumspect in what you write and how you write it. The following very general comments are made in this regard.

Clients

Notes made by you with respect to your conversations with a client (if a third party is *not* present) are probably protected by the attorney–client privilege to the extent that the client is conveying information to you for the purpose of obtaining legal advice.

Witnesses

Notes made by you of an interview with a nonclient witness are not protected by the attorney–client privilege but may or may not be protected as attorney's work product. There is a lot of lore on this.

Other Persons

Notes made by you when you are meeting with persons who are not clients or witnesses, either in negotiations or in conversations, are probably not subject to work product protection. Such notes are certainly not privileged, even though the client may have been present. You should assume that notes of this nature are subject to subpoena. Do not put yourself or your client in the position of being embarrassed by the content of those notes.

Finally, the client himself should be cautioned to protect the attorney–client privilege. Attached as Appendix 4 is a form of letter I use at the beginning of a case to warn a client about the protection of the privilege. This letter, *which needs a lot of refinement*, also warns the client not to destroy documents. This sort of warning is not only necessary for the client's protection; it may be necessary for your own protection.

DEVELOPMENTS IN THE LAW

You should, of course, keep yourself extensively and intensively familiar with developments in the law in the areas in which you work. That's what lawyers are paid for. In a case on which you are working, you should keep yourself and me informed of any new decisions or other developments that bear on the case. It has been my experience that unless one gives an artificial priority to this endeavor, it sits on the back burner. I do not like to be embarrassed by a court's or an adversary's finding a new case before I do.

COURTESY TO STAFF

It goes without saying that no lawyer should ever be rude or overbearing to a staff member. We have a dedicated and supportive staff. We are very fortunate in that regard.

MISCELLANEOUS

I have already referred to the attachment of several appendices. Noted below are two more. They are checklists I prepared long ago for my own use. They may or may not be helpful. They are by no means definitive. They are probably outdated. View them skeptically.

1. Checklist: Taking a Case for a Plaintiff (Appendix 5).
2. Checklist: Taking a Case for a Defendant (Appendix 6).

CONCLUSION

Having said all these things, I say three things in conclusion.

First, unless you seek nothing but personal safety (not a particularly good quality for a lawyer, or anyone else for that matter), there is a reasonable possibility that you will make some mistakes along the way, maybe some serious mistakes. If that comes to pass, try to take comfort in the knowledge that you are not alone. When I first came to New York, many senior New York lawyers (not in my firm) modestly told young associates, "I have never made a mistake." They were not being consciously deceitful. In time, I came to learn that what they were really saying was that their mistakes had never caught up with them and they had repressed the memory thereof.

Second, life is a broader tapestry than the practice of the law. There is a big, wide, wonderful world out there. Don't miss it.

Finally, if you find that any part of this memorandum contains or reflects any erroneous, misleading, scandalous, outmoded, incomplete, or politically incorrect matter or frame of mind, I apologize.

Appendix 1
Checklist: Research

Check sources within the firm (your colleagues, form files, etc.), not only to obtain information but also to avoid duplication or effort:

✓ Consider what law controls: federal, state (which state), or foreign nation (which foreign nation).
✓ Consider whether the matter may be governed in whole or in part by statute, and if so, the possible relevance of legislative history.
✓ Consider whether any regulation, rule, release, or other pronouncement of a regulatory agency governs or bears on the matter. Check the background of the regulation or rule. For example, in the case of SEC regulations and rules, check the various SEC releases that accompanied the proposal, amendment or adoption of the regulation or rule.

When you find a relevant case, follow it through, both backward and forward, by which I mean the following:

1. If there are any citations of earlier decisions, go *backward* to those earlier decisions as well as to any decision of a court below. With respect to each such earlier decision, do the same thing.

2. Then, with respect to each such case, track it *forward*, to identify any case that cites the relevant proposition in your case. Then, with respect to each new case you find going forward, check *that* case backward and forward.

3. Eventually you will find all relevant cases. Obviously, you don't go through all this when you find the answer in a case decided yesterday by the Supreme Court.

✓ Check the history of the case for overruling, reversal, modification, questioning, and so on.

✓ In reading a case for a point of law, always consider how the point of law came up, that is, the procedural context in which it was decided.

✓ When you read a relevant appellate decision, it is usually desirable to read the opinion of the court below. This is particularly important if the case is one that needs to be distinguished. Like appellate advocates, appellate judges tend to describe the facts and holdings below in the manner most favorable to the position they are taking. Thus, an appellate decision may not reflect what the facts really were or what really happened below. The same is true with respect to decisions by administrative agencies such as the SEC or the NLRB. It is often necessary to go to the findings and conclusions of the trial examiner or the hearing examiner.

✓ If you find a case that is helpful or troublesome, it may be desirable to see the briefs that were filed with the court that decided the case. If you cannot otherwise obtain the briefs, you may have to contact the lawyers who were involved in the case.

✓ Make notes as to when the latest updates of research were conducted so that research can be picked up and brought forward at a later time without duplication of effort.

Appendix 2

Brief Writing and Kindred Matters

It is my regret that, at my advanced age, I no longer know and work with as many of you as once I did.

From time to time, however, I am moved to offer advice that I once gave routinely to lawyers working with me. Usually that motivation stems from my being offended by a particular writing. Anyhow, here is the advice. Like most free advice, it is worth just about what you have paid for it.

Whatever may be the styles of law review articles, trust indentures, and the *New York Review of Books* (those styles are much the same), an advocate is not paid or acclaimed (1) for exhibiting skill at using four words when one would do or (2) for demonstrating how many polysyllabic words can be loaded into a multiclause sentence. An advocate is paid and acclaimed for persuasiveness. To that end, short declaratory sentences still live (although sometimes one wonders) and simple words have not been driven out of the English language by complex words and phrases. Why use *carnal convergence* when *sex* will do?

Strunk and White, *The Elements of Style*, along with Fowler's *Modern English Usage*, are part of every literate person's library.

It is not demeaning for you to consult a dictionary. A thesaurus is helpful to avoid repetitious wording. If you are into shades of meaning,

Webster's *Dictionary of Synonyms* is even more help-ful. Bartlett's *Familiar Quotations* and the Bible, par-ticularly the Old Testament, often aid in the sharp-ening of a point. But avoid Shakespeare.

In a brief, the goals are brevity and forcefulness, not the display of erudition. String citations are sus-pect. Long quotations are generally to be avoided. Quoted material is often more effective if it is smoothly woven into the text.

Footnotes in a brief are "an abomination unto the Lord" (*Proverbs* 11:1). They distract the reader and interrupt the flow of argument. I use footnotes only in the following circumstances:

1. when string citations are really necessary or de-sirable,
2. when it is necessary to preserve for the record an argument that I really do not want to make,* or
3. when it is necessary to make myself honest.

In the last regard, it is sometimes desirable to overstate an argument (but not very much) in the text of the brief. A footnote can then be used to make

---

* This often occurs when a client or a colleague insists on making an argument that is not worth making.

qualifications and exceptions that would detract from the flow and forcefulness of argument if they were made in the text.

Humor is sometimes helpful, but it must always be subdued and, even then, must be used with great caution.* The same is true as to idiomatic language.

Litigation is the magazine of the Litigation Section of the ABA. From its beginnings, the magazine has been very successful. It was responsible in great part for the great success of the Litigation Section. The success of the magazine itself stems from the practice of its editors of being utterly ruthless in editing the work of contributors, regardless of who those contributors might be. The editing is often done in personal confrontation. I have seen one of my colleagues, as an editor, participate in that process. He took great glee in it. I have also seen the same colleague, as a contributor, subjected to the same process. He did not like it at all. He pouted (but just a little bit).

As adumbrated (how about *that* for a fancy word?) in the next preceding paragraph (the word

* Many judges are humorous but, often, the only humor they like is their own.

next is redundant), revision is necessary even for the best of writers. A friend and law school classmate of mine, John Biggs III, was the son of John Biggs Jr., a well-known judge on the Third Circuit. Judge Biggs, who was also a competent novelist, was a Princeton classmate and close friend of F. Scott Fitzgerald. When my friend John was born, Fitzgerald wrote a note congratulating the father upon the birth of his first son. The note was a single paragraph, beautifully written. The family said, "Wouldn't it be wonderful to be able to sit down and dash off a sentiment of that nature?" Later, Judge Biggs became Fitzgerald's literary executor. He discovered, in Fitzgerald's papers, that that one short paragraph had gone through seven revisions.

Having said good things about editing and revising, I also say that even good things must come to an end. When a deadline approaches, you simply must stop editing and revising. In that circumstance, if you are editing another person's writing, it is not at all helpful to that person for you to try to recreate the writing in your own image. There is a difference between editing and rewriting.

As I said, even good things must come to an end. Even free advice.

Appendix 3

Rountree Decimal System

PUNICUM BELLUM SECUNDUM LIT.

Index to Files

1.0	Correspondence
2.0	Litigation Record Files
2.1	*Quintus Fabius & Co. v. Hannibal Inc.*, 84 Civ. 5902 (S.D.N.Y.)
2.2	*Hannibal Inc. v. Quintus Fabius & Co.*, 84 Civ. 1234 (S.D. Cal.) [transferred to SDNY and consolidated for pretrial discovery. All future record file filings to be in Record File 2.1]
3.0	Other Record Files
3.1	Memorandum of Fact Record File

    3.1.1   Background Facts: Tyre;
Phoenician Trading; Conflict with Magna
Graecia; Pyhrrus; Sicily: Syracuse: the
Marmetines; the First Confrontation;
Hamilcar Barca; the Peace Party; and all that
    sort of thing [DATE]

    3.1.2   The Events at Saguntum (The Cost of
Pusillanimity) [DATE]

3.2   Memoranda of Law Record File
      3.2.1   Jurisdictional Issues [DATE]
      3.2.2   Disclosure Issues
      3.2.3   Disqualification of Counsel (Termi-
      nation with Extreme Prejudice) [DATE]
4.0   Checklists, Assignments
5.0   Names and Addresses (Parties, Lawyers, Client Personnel, Working Groups, Service Lists, etc.)
5.1   Service List File
5.2   Working Group File
6.0   Billing Information
7.0   Press Releases and Clippings
8.0   Notes
8.1   AR Notes
8.2   SK Notes
9.0   [RESERVED]
10.0   Subject Matter File [Extra Copies of Memo randa of Law and Fact, Etc. (*See* Record Files 3.1 and 3.2. Most material found in the "10" files should also be in 3.1 and 3.2]
10.1   Background facts [DATE]
10.2   Etc.
20.0   Documents (*see also* 71.0, Documents Pro duced by Plaintiff, and 72.0, Documents Pro duced by Defendant)

20.1   The Twelve Tables

20.2   The Sibylline Books

20.3   Schedule 13D of Hannibal Inc.

20.4   Schedule 14D of Hannibal Inc.

50.0   Court Papers Extra *(Quintus Fabius & Co. v. Hannibal Inc.)* [these papers are, by and large, copies of court papers found in Litigation Record File 2.1]

50.1   Summons and Complaint

50.2   Motion for Expedited Discovery and Non-destruction Order

50.3   Motion for Confidentiality Order

50.4   Plaintiff's First Interrogatories

50.5   Plaintiff's First Notice to Produce

50.6   Plaintiff's First Notice of Depositions

50.7   Plaintiff's Motion for Preliminary Injunction

51.0   Court Papers Extra *(Hannibal Inc. v. Quintus Fabius & Co.)* [these papers are, by and large, copies of court papers found in Litigation Record File 2.2]

51.1   Summons and Complaint

51.2   Defendant's Motion to Transfer and to Stay Pending Transfer

70.0   Drafts [It is not necessary to keep every draft of everything. Sometimes it is not prudent to do so.]

Appendix 4

Sample Document: Preservation Letter to Client

[Date]

PRIVILEGED & CONFIDENTIAL

To: Troy Incorporated

      Rex J. Priam

      Don John Paris

      Helen Menelaus

      J.J. ("Foots") Hector

Agamemnon Associates v. Troy Incorporated

Gentlefolks:

Although it may be unnecessary in the case of you sophisticated, litigious tigers, we offer the initial advice we give to all clients at the commencement of a lawsuit.

1. You should not destroy any documents that relate to this matter. If you do so, you risk a criminal charge of obstruction of justice. In addition, the trier of fact may be permitted to draw adverse inferences from such destruction. [**You may want to describe the categories of documents that relate to this matter.**]

2. Any oral or written communications, and any other writings, that relate to the subject matter of this litigation and are not subject to the attorney–client privilege may be discoverable by plaintiff. You should be careful to preserve the attorney–client privilege. In this regard, we note the following:

   (a) Any conversations that you or your personnel have among yourselves, or with others, outside the presence of counsel, may be subject to discovery.

   (b) Any notes or other writings that you or your

personnel prepare, except writings directed to this firm for the purpose of seeking legal advice, may be subject to discovery. Generally speaking, no such writing should be prepared except at our specific request. Copies of any such writings should be kept in a special file to which only restricted personnel have access, and the file should be marked confidential. Copies should not be distributed.

(c) Writings that you receive from us should be kept in the same file. Copies should not be made or distributed.

(d) Any advice or information that we give to you should not be disclosed to others.

3. Enclosed are more comprehensive instructions with respect to the protection of the attorney–client privilege. [*Editor's note*: For example, you may want to provide special instructions concerning the preservation and/or segregation of files of, or communications with, particular lawyers involved in the matter; or explain that business advice (as distinguished from legal advice) provided by in-house counsel or any other attorney is not privileged.]

4. If you have any questions about any of this, please get in touch with us.

You may truly believe us, dear folks, when we say that we are, as ever,

Your Obedient Servants,

Appendix 5

Checklist:
Taking a Case for a Plaintiff

The matters contained herein relate to considerations to be had, thoughts to be thunk, during the initial stages of an action in which we are asked to represent a plaintiff. Some of the matters relate to the further handling of the case, but only incidentally.

1. The Initial Interview
Immediately advise the client of the nature *and limits* of the attorney–client privilege. Advise the client of what he should do to protect the attorney–client privilege. Get the facts. In the course of getting the facts, be sensitive to the possibility of conflicts. In many situations, you have to check the conflict situation before even getting into the facts.

2. Whether to Take Case

All of the circumstances should be considered, including the following:

a. The nature and character of the client. Will he be honest, reasonably available as necessary, and not impossible to work with? Will he heed our instructions and pay our bills?

b. The justness of the cause.

c. Is there any conflict of interest? If so, is it waivable and can a waiver be obtained?

d. Do we have the requisite expertise? Can the case be properly staffed?

e. Fee arrangements. Can the client afford us and can we afford the client? Is the case one where the legal cost will be disproportionate to the amount in controversy? If so then the client should determine whether he really wants to prosecute the case and, if so, whether he might not get cheaper service elsewhere. If the client wants to fight for principle, be sure he is willing to pay for principle. Establish an understanding as to when bills will be submitted to the client.

3. Attorney–Client Privilege

After deciding to take the case, again focus on the attorney–client privilege and its limitations. [See Appendix 4.]

4. *Whether to Commence an Action*

Initially, consideration should be given as to whether it is necessary or desirable to commence an action at all.

a. Is it worthwhile to attempt negotiation before commencing the action or will this simply allow the defendant to take the initiative?

b. Is arbitration, mediation, or some other form of ADR available, and, even if so, is it desirable? If the action is to be based on a contract containing an arbitration clause, what are the odds that the other side will invoke the arbitration clause if we commence an action?

c. If an action is brought, does it create the situation in which the client will be submitted to counterclaims that could not, or might not, otherwise be asserted? In this regard, be particularly careful about filing claims in a bankruptcy proceeding, particularly if the client has received a preference. If he files a claim, he will submit himself to the jurisdiction of the Bankruptcy Court. Is there any risk of a claim of malicious prosecution or abuse of process?

5. *When to Commence the Action*

In considering when to bring the action, take the following into account:

a. Do we have authority to commence the action?

b. The statute of limitations. When does the statute run? If it is about to run, move fast. Amend later.

c. If the statute may run in a short time, consider whether we can do anything to toll the running of the statute. In some states, a summons can be filed with the sheriff. We may be able to negotiate a tolling agreement with the defendant. Consider whether tolling agreement is valid. It may be necessary to take risk.

6. *Where to Commence the Action*

In choosing the forum, if there is a choice, consider the following:

a. What will be the governing substantive law?

b. In what jurisdictions can we obtain personal jurisdiction over the defendant?

c. Does the court have any jurisdictional requirements with respect to amount in controversy?

d. Do we have a choice between federal court and state court? If we can go into federal court, is the applicable federal law or one circuit more favorable than the law of another circuit, and can we get personal jurisdiction in the circuit in which the law is most favorable?

e. Is the procedural law, including the statute of limitations, more favorable in one jurisdiction than in another?

f. What is the expense of litigation in one forum as compared to another?

g. What is the usual time to trial or judgment in one forum as compared to another?

7. *Actual Commencement of the Action*

In actually commencing the action, take the following into account:

a. Does any preliminary demand or notice have to be made or given to the defendant or anyone else? For example, in some states, an attack upon the constitutionality of a state statute has to be preceded by notice to the Attorney General of the state.

b. Be familiar with the rules and requirements for filing in the particular court in which the action is to be filed.

c. Do we want a jury trial? It may be that demand has to be made in the initial pleading or a jury is deemed to have been waived.

8. *Preliminary or Extraordinary Relief*

Consider whether preliminary or extraordinary relief is necessary or desirable:

a. Is defendant about to flee the jurisdiction? Are his assets about to disappear? Is he about to commit an act that will result in irreparable injury?

b. Is there any self-help that needs to be taken? What are the risks?

c. Are such remedies as arrest, attachment, receivership, or injunction available? If so, take into account the costs and risks. For example:

(i) A bond will probably have to be posted.

(ii) In attachment proceedings, poundage fees run high.

(iii) If an *ex parte* restraining order is obtained and is later dissolved as being improvidently granted, the client may be subjected to the payment of damages.

9. *Notice of Commencement of Action*

Do we have to give any notice to anyone of the commencement of the action? For example:

a. to an insurer?

b. under a contract requirement?

c. to the Securities and Exchange Commission (see, e.g., the Investment Company Act)?

d. to any other regulatory agency?

e. through the filing of a Form 8K?

f. to the New York or other stock exchange?

g. through a press release to the general public?

h. to the client's auditors?

If notice has to be given, then pay attention to the mechanics of the giving of the notice, particularly if a press release has to be given.

10. *Service of Process*
Make arrangements for service of process. Determine whether quick service has to be effected.

11. *Initial Discovery*
Decide whether, generally, to take an aggressive or a passive posture in discovery. Consider whether the relevant court has special procedures or rules that govern discovery. For example, in state court, consider whether it is necessary to do anything in order to obtain and retain any priority of discovery.

12. Keeping Client Informed

Determine the extent to which the client wants to be kept informed about the progress of the case. Is there anyone else, such as an insurer or codefendant, who should be kept informed? Establish procedures for keeping people informed.

Appendix 6

Checklist: Taking a Case for a Defendant

The matters contained herein relate to considerations to be had during the initial stages of an action in which we are asked to represent a defendant. Some of the matters relate to the further handling of the case, but only incidentally.

1. The Initial Interview

Immediately advise the client of the nature *and limits* of the attorney–client privilege. Advise the client of what he should do to protect the attorney–client privilege. Get the facts. In the course of getting the facts, be sensitive to the possibility of conflicts. In many situations, you have to check the conflict situation before even getting into the facts.

2. Whether to Take Case

All of the circumstances should be considered, including the following:

a. The nature and character of the client. Will he be honest, reasonably available as necessary, and not impossible to work with? Will he heed our instructions and pay our bills?
b. The justness of the cause.
c. Is there any conflict of interest? If so, is it waivable and can a waiver be obtained?
d. Do we have the requisite expertise? Can the case be properly staffed?
e. Fee arrangements. Can the client afford us and can we afford the client? Is the case one where the legal cost will be disproportionate to the amount in controversy? If so, then the client should determine whether he really wants to prosecute the case and, if so, whether he might not get cheaper service elsewhere. If the client wants to fight for principle, be sure he is willing to pay for principle. Establish an understanding as to when bills will be submitted to the client.

3. Attorney –Client Privilege

After deciding to take the case, again focus on the attorney–client privilege and its limitations. [See Appendix 4.]

4. Whether to Attempt to Forestall Action

Consider whether it is feasible or desirable to attempt to forestall or, on the other hand, to precipitate litigation.

a. Is it worthwhile to attempt to talk the plaintiff out of commencing the action against our client? This works more often than one would think.
b. Are there collateral pressures which can properly be brought to bear on this evil person who is making menacing gestures at our client?
c. Is a preemptive strike feasible and desirable? This may be particularly important
   (i) if the substantive or procedural law of one jurisdiction is more favorable than that of another,
   (ii) if the expense of litigation in one forum is different from that of another, or

(iii) if there is any real psychological advantage to be gained by taking aggressive action.

d. Is arbitration, mediation, or some other form of ADR available and, if so, is it desirable to attempt to have the matter adjudicated by an arbitrator? My own experience (at least in commercial arbitration as distinguished from labor arbitration) is that unless one has a real loser of a case and therefore is willing to roll the dice, arbitration is disastrous.

5. Initial Appearance

Be sure that you have authority to appear for a client. Often, it is desirable to have this authority set forth in writing. If an attorney appears and submits a client to the jurisdiction of the court without having authority, it can lead to dire consequences for the attorney.

6. Procedures and Defenses

Consider the following matters in connection with an initial appearance in the case. Be sure to take no steps that constitute a waiver of available defenses:

a. Be familiar with the rules of the particular court. Don't make guesses about the procedures of the court.

b. Determine when and upon whom service of process was effected, not only to calculate time of response to the complaint, but also to determine whether the service of process was defective and can be set aside.

c. By what date must a response be made to the summons or complaint?

d. If the action is brought in state court, do we want to remove to federal court and, if so, what is the time limit for so doing?

e. What defenses have to be made initially or will be deemed to be waived?

   (i) absence of personal jurisdiction,

   (iii) venue,

   (iii) etc.

f. Are initial defenses to be made by motion or set forth in an answer?

g. Consider whether stipulation as to extension of time to move or answer will submit the client to the jurisdiction of the court.

h. Are any counterclaims, crossclaims, or third party claims to be made? Be very careful about time limits. Be very careful about compulsory counter-claims or crossclaims.

i. Is there anyone who should be "vouched in" [i.e., by appearance *pro hac vice*] to defend the action on behalf of the client?

j. Can the action be stayed on grounds of
(i) arbitration,
(ii) another action already pending,
(iii) other grounds?

k. Can we move for security for costs?

l. Do we want to demand a jury? If so, when does this have to be done?

m. Has the plaintiff failed to make a necessary preliminary demand?

n. Has the statute of limitations run?

o. Are there any other affirmative defenses?

7. *Notice of Commencement of Action*

Do we have to give any notice to anyone of the commencement of the action? For example:

a. to an insurer or other indemnitor? [Be careful to do nothing that will jeopardize a claim to indemnity.]

b. under a contract requirement?

c. to the Securities and Exchange Commission (see, e.g., under the Investment Company Act)?

d. to any other regulatory agency?

e. by the filing of a Form 8-K?

f. to the New York or other stock exchange?

g. by a press release to the general public?

h. to the client's auditors?

If notice has to be given, then pay attention to the mechanics of the giving of the notice, particularly if a press release has to be given.

8. Initial Discovery

Decide, generally, whether to take an aggressive or passive posture in discovery. Consider whether the relevant court has special procedures or rules that govern discovery. For example, in state court, consider whether it is necessary to do anything in order to obtain and retain any priority to take discovery.

9. Other Preliminary Matters

a. Is it feasible and desirable to move to disqualify the attorneys for the plaintiff?

b. If our client has a claim for indemnity or contribution against a person in bankruptcy, determine whether a contingency claim has to be filed in the bankruptcy proceeding and, if so, when.

CHAPTER TWO

The Settlement of Disputes

Whether, When, and How to Settle a Legal Dispute

In a legal context, settlement is the consensual disposition of a dispute without a binding adjudication by a court or arbitrator. The consent need not be friendly; generally, it is not. It's just a consent.

DISPUTE ANALYSIS

It would be endless to dispute
everything that is disputable.
~ William Penn

One would think that a dispute is merely a dispute. Not so. Analysis reveals that disputes are born of real or imagined injuries and grow to adulthood somewhat as follows:

1. An injury is suffered or is perceived to have been suffered. A grievance may or may not follow.
2. A grievance arises when the injured person perceives, rightly or wrongly, that someone else is

responsible for his injury. A claim may or may not follow. The injured party may, for example, turn the other cheek; he may merely grouse; he may go for the jugular; he may bide his time waiting for a quiet revenge; or he may assert a claim.

3. A claim is a demand for redress. The response by the alleged wrongdoer may be
   a. acquiescence,
   b. an offer of compromise (settlement), or
   c. rejection of the claim.
4. If the claim is rejected, then the injured party has the options of
   a. acquiescence,
   b. self-help, or
   c. appeal to the courts or some other tribunal.

At any stage of the process, a lawyer may be introduced to consider whether an injury has in fact occurred and, if so, whether there is legal redress; to advise whether to assert a claim and, if so, when and where and against whom; to advise whether to litigate or settle the claim; to handle the litigation or settlement; or generally to make a nuisance of himself.

WHETHER TO SETTLE A DISPUTE

Blessed are the peacemakers,
for they shall be called the children of God.
~ Matthew 5:9

Should a dispute be settled? This question, asked in the abstract, can only be answered Yes. Disputes should be settled as quickly, as fairly, and as amicably as possible. Society demands no less. But what I address here is whether a dispute, once it is in litigation or is on the threshold thereof, should be settled. This determination can be made in diverse ways: by rational analysis, by intuition, by experience, by divination, or by rolling the dice, to name just a few.

In theory at least, the client, not the lawyer, decides whether to try to settle a dispute. The lawyer just recommends. In deciding whether to recommend settlement, the lawyer takes into account a number of factors. For example:

1. The lawyer must make an assessment of his client's likelihood of prevailing. In making this assessment he must take into account such factors as the likely evidence, the unlikely evidence, the law, the capriciousness of judges and juries, the capacities

of opposing counsel, and the vagaries of time and chance.

2. The lawyer must take into account the extent of his client's exposure, financial or otherwise, if the client does not prevail.

3. The lawyer must take into account the financial ability of his client to submit himself to such exposure. A $10 million judgment will not destroy General Motors; it would be disconcerting to the corner grocer.

4. The lawyer must take into account the emotional ability of the client to submit himself to the risk of exposure. Some clients are high rollers who enjoy the thrill of playing "bet-your-company." Others are risk averse. Know thy client.

5. The lawyer must take into account any collateral effects of the disposition of the dispute, for example, the effect of a settlement or adverse adjudication as a precedent or the effect of the disposition on any possibility or desire of the client to continue to do business with his adversary.

6. There are those who say that the lawyer must take into account the public weal in deciding whether to recommend settlement to his client. I do not

really subscribe to that view myself, but the times may have passed me by.

One thing a lawyer must *not* take into account is his own emotion: his antipathy toward opposing counsel, his identification with or repugnance for the cause, his desire to flex his muscles, his fear of trying the case. Unfortunately, many cases are settled because the lawyer is afraid to try the case. He might lose; still worse, he might look bad.

WHEN TO SETTLE A DISPUTE

*To everything there is a season,
and a time to every purpose under heaven.*
~ Ecclesiastes 3:1

If a decision is made to try to settle, when should the attempt first be made? Before litigation is commenced? Early in litigation? Before discovery? After discovery? In the midst of trial? While the jury is deliberating? After judgment but before appeal? Well, to use a military expression, it all depends on the situation and the terrain. That's not very helpful, but here are some miscellaneous observations in no particular order of importance.

1. In deciding when to settle, one must make an estimate as to whether the price will go up or down with time. In short, when do you figure you can get the best deal? Does the plaintiff need money now? Does his attorney? When will the smoking gun surface? And what will that do to the price of settlement?

2. It is fashionable to say these days that lawyers prolong litigation and delay settlement in order to run up large legal fees. It has been my experience, at least from the standpoint of representing defendants, that this simply is not so. More often than not, it is the client who resists settlement. There is often a complex background to the litigation. Perhaps there are charges of fraud. Emotions have run high, positions have been taken, and face must be saved.

3. For these reasons, a lawyer must often be very careful in approaching his client about settlement. The client may think that the lawyer is timid or has sold out to the powers of evil. The lawyer must be careful as to how he presents the weaknesses in the client's case. Always he must assure the client that he is willing to fight, is on the client's side, and that the other folks are evil folks, but that the

client's self-interest and rationality, as well as the prospect of not wasting more time on the likes of those folks, dictate that the client at least consider settlement.

4. Don't misunderstand me. Many clients approach a case in a very realistic way. They say, "I don't care if that fellow has called me a thief and a scoundrel. I've been called worse. I am worse. It's just business. I have better things to do than waste time with him and with you, too, for that matter. I don't care whether you try the case or settle the case. Just get me out of it as quick as you can and as cheap as you can." Such clients are a joy unto the spirit of the lawyer.

5. Many lawyers believe that to be the first to broach settlement is to display fatal weakness. Sometimes this is true, sometimes not, but many superb lawyers and many experienced clients believe this always to be true.

6. Is it ever proper for a lawyer to explore settlement with his adversary without first obtaining the permission of his client? Some clients will fire you if you do so. Other clients will give you strict instructions not to, then fire you if you don't. Oh well, clients are clients.

WHO SHOULD SETTLE A DISPUTE

Woe unto you also, ye lawyers,
for ye lade men with burdens grievous to be borne,
and ye yourselves touch not the burdens
with one of your fingers.
~ Luke 11:46

Generally, settlement negotiations should be conducted by the lawyer, who, of course, should keep his client informed. Generally, the client should not be present. For one thing, this gives the lawyer more flexibility. Occasionally, one side or the other will suggest that the clients meet alone without the lawyers. Occasionally, this is a good idea, but there are dangers, and the client should be so advised. Never should the lawyer permit his ego to stand in the way of such a meeting.

On the rarest of occasions, a client will want to negotiate directly with opposing counsel without the presence of his own lawyer. This is permissible only with the consent of the lawyer who is to be absent. The excluded lawyer ought not to go off in a pout about this.

I consider below the introduction into the settlement process of outsiders such as judges, mediators,

settlement experts, intermediaries, officious intermediaries, and the like.

HOW TO SETTLE A DISPUTE

Ask, and it shall be given you; seek and ye shall find;
knock and it shall be opened unto you.
~ Matthew 7:7

In negotiations, feelings of revenge or hatred
or desire for compensation for injury suffered
are very poor guides.
In negotiations, I believe, one should be guided
by correlation of forces.
~ Joseph Stalin*

Negotiation

Negotiation was once considered to be an art. Either
you had it or you did not. Today, negotiation, like
most everything else, is subjected to endless analysis. It appears now that there are basically two types
of bargaining:

* Stalin is also said once to have said, "The Pope? How many divisions
does *he* have?" The Pope is said to have replied, "Tell my son Joseph
that he shall meet my divisions in Heaven." (Or somewhere.)

1. Bargaining that is variously referred to as cooperative bargaining, problem-solving bargaining, principled bargaining, integrative bargaining, win-win bargaining, or the like. In this type of bargaining, the bargainer does not try to maximize the return to his client. He tries to come out with the right result, whatever that may be.

2. Bargaining that is variously referred to as competitive bargaining, distributional bargaining, power bargaining, zero-sum bargaining, or the like. In this type of bargaining each bargainer seeks to obtain more at the expense of the other.

Legal academicians are enamored of the first type of bargaining. Perhaps that is why they are academicians. Clients, on the other hand, usually think they are paying legal practitioners for the second type of bargaining.* One should bear in mind an incident, highly publicized, in which a Chicago lawyer was fired for having engaged in unauthorized "cooperative" bargaining. The cli-

---

* In cases where the issues are public in nature, as distinguished from grubby private issues (like money), there is much to be said for the first type of bargaining.

ent is said to have said, as he threw the lawyer down the stairs, "Why, you pusillanimous, limicolous little wimp, if I had wanted to give my money away, I would have hired a tax lawyer or a public relations man, not a trial lawyer."

I make no attempt in this paper to go into bargaining tactics. A lawyer holds onto that sort of lore like a squirrel holds onto his nuts. I do mention some general rules that are touted by one Robert F. Hanley, Esq., who was an eminent trial lawyer and a man of many parts in many places:

1. Don't settle too early.
2. Don't settle too late.
3. Try not to settle piecemeal. Try to get rid of the whole case.
4. Divide and conquer, particularly if you are a plaintiff.
5. Test your adversary's trial eagerness. Does that tiger really want to go to trial? Has he ever tried a case? How many? How long ago? How will he play before a jury composed of an unemployed longshoreman, an illiterate janitor, a single mother on welfare, a postal worker, and a shoe clerk? How well will *you* play before that kind of jury?

6. Be prepared. Be prepared. Be prepared. Have a solid grasp of your factual and legal theories before you discuss settlement.
7. Test the state of your opponent's personal preparation. Not his law firm's preparation, not his bright young associate's preparation, but his preparation. If he doesn't really know his case, you are in a good position in settlement negotiations to capitalize on your own preparation.
8. If you have a good case, consider pressing for an early trial and consider seeking judicial intervention in the settlement process.

Countless intriguing questions arise about the negotiation process. For example: Does a lawyer ever make his best and final offer first? Very seldom. Is it ever ethically permissible to lie (or at least to shade the truth) in the course of negotiations? Is it permissible, for example, to lie about the extent of your authority, or about whether your last and final offer is really your last and final offer? Those are difficult questions. Is it ever permissible to attempt to "go around" the other lawyer and indirectly reach his client? No. Is it ever desirable to try to settle cases over drinks? It depends on how well you hold your liquor. How often are negotiations determined by the physical stamina of the parties? Often.

HOW TO CONSUMMATE THE SETTLEMENT

For where your treasure is, there will your heart be also.
~ Matthew 6:21

Bring money.
~ Perry Goldberg

Timing

Once a settlement has been agreed upon, it is usually desirable to memorialize it in a Settlement Agreement as soon as possible, although sometimes, even with large amounts of money, it is sufficient simply to pay the money, get a release, file a stipulation of dismissal, and go hence. But whatever may be the means, it is usually desirable to button up the settlement quickly. The Pennzoil-Getty-Texaco triangle is a dramatic example of the importance of speed. Pennzoil sought Getty's hand in holy wedlock. Getty said yes. The banns were published. But before the lawyers could prepare the marriage contract, Texaco

slipped into the lady's bedroom. It has been sug-
gested, rightly or wrongly, that if the papers had been
prepared more quickly, Getty's window would have
been closed when Texaco came serenading that long
lost, moon-burning night.

The Settlement Documents

1. *The Wherewithal.* The most important papers exchanged in the consummation of a settlement are usually colored green. However, cases
are often settled for consideration other than
money. Cases can be settled by the exchange of
property, by the issuance of stock, by entering into
agreements to do business in the future (although
not in violation of the antitrust laws), by including an apology, indeed by a myriad of ingenious
devices, some known and some not yet dreamed
of. In negotiating settlements, one must never
overlook such possibilities.

2. *The Settlement Agreement.* Usually, as I have
said, a written Settlement Agreement sets forth the
consideration to be paid, the method of payment,
the mechanics and place and time of closing, the form

of the releases to be given or exchanged, a disclaimer of liability, a designation of governing law, and often all sorts of other things.

3. *Releases.* A release is almost always given. Often releases are exchanged. The release can be a general release or a special (limited) release.

You should in every instance check the state law applicable to the release. Sometimes releases do not really cover what they say they cover. Also, in giving a release, be sure that you are not releasing others. In some states, unless certain precautions are taken, a release of one joint tortfeasor will release all other joint tortfeasors.

4. *Stipulation of Dismissal.* If the settlement concerns a pending action, a Stipulation and Order of Dismissal must be entered into.

Settlement by Less Than All Defendants

In a multidefendant case, if you represent a defendant who is settling when other defendants are not settling, you must take steps to protect your clients from claims for contribution or indemnity. Be sure to check the applicable state law regarding how best to protect your client from any further claims by a codefendant once the client has settled.

Other Matters

There follow here some other matters to be taken into account:

1. It may be important to your client that the terms of a settlement—sometimes even the fact of the settlement itself—be kept confidential. This should be covered in the Settlement Agreement and by whatever other means may be appropriate and proper.
2. You may want to include a covenant not to sue. It may be useful because its breach may give rise to a separate action for damages. Further protection is afforded if the covenant provides for recovery of attorney's fees if the covenant is breached.
3. If the defendant is insured, approval by the carrier must be obtained before the defendant agrees to a settlement.
4. You should always consider the tax consequences of a settlement. It may be that a different structure will result in more favorable tax consequences.

CONCLUSION

It begins in delight and ends in wisdom.
~ Robert Frost

Well, more or less.

CHAPTER THREE

Vacation Memorandum
[Limited Edition]

I shall be at Ponte Vedra Beach, where I shall be painting canvases. In the artistic world, I am known as R. Brant (the "R" stands for Rhemm). For those of you who are collectors, I have listed the offerings of The Magnus, the exclusive distributor of Brant paintings.

THE MAGNUS GALLERY
875 Third Avenue
New York, NY 10022

Offering Nos.: PV-1, PV-2, PV-3, PV-4, PV-5
Work: The Ponte Vedra Sequence (R. Brant, 1990)
Prices: Price negotiations begin only upon receipt by us of a bid made by wire transfer of federal funds

Having disappeared for 18 months, Brant was found living in a castle by the sea at a place called Ponte Vedra. The castle was owned by Brant, his creditors, and three mistresses (the creditors' mistresses, not Brant's; Brant doesn't cotton to that sort of thing). Anyhow, the mistresses had taken after the creditors, the creditors had taken after Brant, and so Brant had to take to painting again. Then he took the paintings to us and we now take them to you, in all their artistic and costly elegance.

PV-1: **A Summer Sky**

In the San Francisco Earthquake of 1906, an early Brant painting, "A Summer Sky," was destroyed. It broke Brant's heart. This year, Brant, still nursing his broken heart in that castle by the sea (Brant likes to nurse these things), decided to paint the painting once again. So here it is: a cobalt blue sky, visible behind a screen of white clouds that are so delicate that Brant had to paint them with an egret feather instead of a brush. Still, Brant's broken heart will be mended only if you break your pocketbook by buying this painting.

PV2: **A Sharp Incline**

In the San Francisco Earthquake of 1989, another Brant painting was destroyed. This painting, however, was one about which Brant had ambiguous feelings (Magnus Offering No. M-E-B-43). Sometimes Brant called it "A Sharp Incline." Sometimes he called it "A Sharp Decline." In the fullness of his years, Brant has decided on "A Sharp Incline" and has repainted the painting in that spirit. The painting still represents Brant's most successful excursion into explicit symbolism, a mode in which Brant is not as much at home as with essentialistic obscurantism.

PV3: **Thrice in a Blue Moon**

One blue moon was not enough for Brant. He painted three of them. He figured he could get three times as much money for three blue moons as he could for one blue moon. That Brant, he's a real mathematician.

PV4: **Shark's Tooth**

Back in 1917, when Brant was raiding with T.E. Lawrence in Arabia, he came across a ruined temple of Poseidon. How was it that a temple to the Sea God of the Hellenes had been built in the middle of the Arabian desert? Brant didn't ponder upon that question because Brant does not ponder upon much of anything. He simply spied in the center of the sacred altar a sacred fossilized shark's tooth. Brant then stole it. Now, years later, when Brant figures that Poseidon has forgotten about him (although Brant still keeps a wary eye out whenever he is by the sea), Brant has mounted the shark's tooth on a titanium white canvas, where it is faintly accentuated by symmetrical lines of cerulean blue. (The only color Brant likes better than the color of blue is the color of green.) You should be aware that the shark's tooth is two million years old. Two million. Does that suggest a price to you? Well, it might do for an opening bid. Remember, only a few weeks ago a tradesman from Japan paid $86.5 million for some dried oil on canvas. A fossilized shark's tooth will last a lot longer than dried oil. It will last longer than canvas, too. Or Brant. Or you.

PV-5: **The Sun over the Sea at Two O'clock Post Meridian**

This painting is nostalgic of Brant's famous "The Sun at Noonday" (Magnus Offering No. XY-26). Now, the sun, like Brant, is older. Like Brant, it is beyond its zenith, although, like Brant, it is still high in the sky and it still burns with intensity and ferocity. Beneath it, far beneath it, the great shroud of the sea rolls on as it rolled a billion years ago. That's right, a billion. But not to worry. We are not talking about that kind of money. Not yet.

You better hustle on in. That great art connoisseur Donald Trump may get here before you do, unless the high rollers down in Atlantic City do him in first.

CHAPTER FOUR

Request for Expense Reimbursement

REINC

Willy Loman, Esq.
Chief Hustler and Dispenser
of Expense Account Largess
Debevoise & Plimpton
875 Third Avenue
New York, NY 10022

Request for Expense Reimbursement
for Attendance at Annual Meeting
of Litigation Section, Washington, DC

Dear Squire Loman:

You may wonder why I am writing on REINC letter-head for a D&P expense reimbursement. Let me explain. I have an arrangement whereby I assign all of my accounts receivable and all of my accounts payable to REINC. REINC then collects the accounts receivable and immediately dividends out the cash to its sole stock-holder. Then REINC stalls on the accounts payable. It demands documentation. It claims breach of warranty. It sends unsigned checks. It says that checks must have been lost in the mails. When all else fails, REINC simply defaults. Creditors then turn to me. I look at them with my big blue eyes and run my fingers through my curly blond hair and say, gee, ah, well, after all, I assigned everything to REINC. I then assign to my creditors all my claims against REINC. That satisfies most of them. With off-setting debits and credits, they are happy. But when enough of them get sufficiently unhappy, then REINC and I do a Long Gone Jones act. REINC is incorporated in many jurisdictions. I have residences in many places.

Anyhow, Willy, I submit herewith my accounting for expenses incurred in attending the ABA Litigation Section's annual meeting in Washington. I attended in my capacity as former Chairman of the Litigation Section. I done good, too, Willy. I patted all the things I was supposed to pat, and I kept my hands off all those things I was not supposed to pat.

You can search that account all you want to, Willy, and you won't find no $5 cigars and you won't find no $500 women. (It never cost that much back in the old days, believe me.) That reminds me of another story. Perhaps I have told it to you before. It happens at my age. That reminds me of something else. I once had a friend who had the marvelous capacity of being unable to remember the stories I told her. Being a New Yorker, you probably don't know what that means to a storyteller — having a constantly attentive audience, but not having to make up new material. But then this woman miraculously recovered her memory. It was as if the Angel of the Lord had come to visit her (she did keep good company), because one day she said, "Listen, Rountree, if I have heard that story once, I've heard it ten times." Something told me that romance was over.

Anyhow, you won't find cigars or women in *my* expense account. Now, you may find a few alcohol stains in the paper work. But that's what these affairs are all about. People who succeed in these organizations, and form networks which later produce business, do so not because they are good lawyers or faithful servants, but because they can drink more and stay up longer than other folks (or at least they give the appearance of being able to do so).

Anyhow, Willy, you can approve or disapprove or increase or decrease this request in any way you see fit. I have unlimited faith in your generosity, your parsimony, your judgment, and your charity,

Sincerely yours,
Asa Rountree

Enclosures [intentionally omitted]

CHAPTER FIVE

The Section of Litigation

It is hard to believe how much time has passed since the founding of the Litigation Section in 1973. Will Wright, a single practitioner in Houston, Texas, was the driving force behind the founding of the Section. Single-handedly, and at his own expense, he went around the country putting together the group that might be said to be the founders of the Section, including Bob Hanley, Paul Connolly, Bill Manning, George Meisel, Ron Olson, Lee Cooper, and myself. That group included, in great part, lawyers who had never been particularly active in the ABA and wanted to form a section that would be free of the bureaucratic strictures of the mother organization. In that, they were successful for a number of years.

George Meisel of Cleveland was the Section's first chairman. He brought to the job a maturity and soundness of judgment without which the Section might not have succeeded. (The newly formed Section was not very popular with the hierarchy of the ABA.) Will Wright, who was somewhat more flamboyant than George Meisel, was the second chairman. Will was a better creator and organizer than he was an administrator. The Section was really institutionalized by its third chairman, Bob Hanley.

In the fall of the second year of the Section's existence, during the chairmanship of Will Wright, an organizational meeting of officers, council members, and committee chairmen was held one weekend in Chicago. A number of constructive things may have been done, but the weekend was mostly memorable (to those who could remember it at all) as a wonderful party. After that weekend, a committee chairman from California went home and commenced to write the president of the ABA and members of its Board of Governors saying that this group was not any proper section of the American Bar Association but was just a bunch of drinking buddies who had gotten together. That was disturbing to me. I called Bob Hanley and said, "What are we going to do about this?" Bob said, "Don't worry about it. I have already taken care of it." I said, "What do you mean you have taken care of it?" Bob said, "I called that fellow and told him to go chase himself." (The infinitive phrase used by Bob was much stronger.)

In the summer of 1978, at the annual ABA meeting, which that year was in New York, the Section gave its dinner dance at the Guggenheim Museum. It was the first time, I believe, that a New York museum had made its facilities available for that sort of affair. Earlier, New York museums had made their facilities available for parties given by very big donors, but not to persons or organizations not otherwise connected with the museum. The affair was successful, not only from the standpoint of the Litigation Section but also from the financial standpoint of the museum. Since that time, the museums of New York have been deriving substantial revenues from allowing their facilities to be used for parties. I have always thought that they owe the Litigation Section a commission.

Some time during Phil Corboy's chairmanship, when I was chairman-elect, I attended the annual meeting of section chairmen. Corboy did not have much use for meetings of that kind. He considered them a waste of time. I was of the same persuasion, but somebody from the Section had to attend. Just before that event, one of the Section's committee chairmen had made a presentation to a congressional committee that took a position contrary to the ABA position on a particular issue. As chairman-elect and as the representative of the Litigation Section, I was excoriated by a high ABA official. I was told that the Section should discipline the committee chairman by removing him from office and that the Section should apologize to the ABA and take an oath in blood that the Section would never again do a thing like that. My response was that the Section would not remove the chairman. I said, "You have to understand that the Litigation Section, like its chairman and its chairman-elect, is young and undisciplined." We heard no more of the matter.

In the early days of the Section, succession to the chairmanship was decided by incumbent members of the leadership. When it came my time, either as vice chairman or as chairman-elect, to select a nomination committee, I called up Lee Cooper and said, "Lee, what would you think about Bud Foley as chairman of the Section?" Lee said, "I think that is a great idea." I said, "Lee, how would you like to serve on the nomination committee?" It is my understanding that the chairman of the Section is now chosen by more democratic means.

My term (1980-1981) was not notable for any great accomplishments. The Section's committee on discovery abuse, which had been formed and chaired by Wey Lundquist, continued its work. The Section devoted considerable attention to various proposals to establish minimum standards of trial competence and to promote excellence in trial performances. The Section also turned its attention to the phenomenon of the so-called complex case. Among other things, the Section devised a study that was intended, through an elaborate post-verdict interview process, to obtain empirical data concerning whether jurors really understand the issues in complex litigation. A committee to study punitive damages was also appointed.

But my most important goal as chairman was to try to bring some discipline to the finances and budgeting of the Section. I think I was successful. When Ron Olson succeeded me as chairman, he said that the goal of his administration would be to "spend like Corboy and save like Rountree."

Whenever I think of the Litigation Section, I think of Harrison Tweed's words which are carved on the wall in the entrance hall of the the Association of the Bar of the City of New York: "I have a high opinion of lawyers. With all their faults, they stack up well against those in every other occupation or profession. They are better to work with or play with or fight with or drink with than most other varieties of mankind."

CHAPTER SIX

On Name Changes

Henceforth my name is Asa Rountree (in whom I am well pleased). No more of this "J" foolishness.

Actually, no change of name is involved, just a reselection from an abundant inventory of existing names. When I applied for admission to the New York Bar, the questionnaire included a question: "Have you ever been known by any other name?" My response was along the following lines:

I have been known by many names at many places. I have been known as Asa Rountree. I have been known as Asa Rountree III. I have been known as John Rountree, John Rountree III, John A. Rountree, John A. Rountree III, J. Asa Rountree, J. Asa Rountree III, and John Asa Rountree. To the delight of top sergeants taking predawn roll call, I have been known as John Asa Rountree [pause, giggle] the Thoid. I have been judicially referred to as Asa J. Rountree III, *Wright v. City of Tuscaloosa,* 236 Ala. 374, 182 So. 72, 77 (1938) ("little Asa" in the lower court), and for years in Tuscaloosa, Alabama, I was known to and loved by all as "Sonny." None of this is to mention the several road names of a dissolute youth. Nor is this to mention the rich variations of Rountree and Asa, such as Squaretree, Squarebush, Ace, Acie, Assa, and others I blush to recall.

If You Knew Asa

I had the good fortune of working with Asa during most of the decade after I arrived at Debevoise, Plimpton, Lyons & Gates in 1978. On countless occasions it has crossed my mind that decisions I was making, ranging from filing a motion to deleting a comma, were influenced by something Asa had said or done. But it's hard for me to say what I learned from Asa about litigating. There's too much to remember or to recount.

I'll try it this way. For the most part, Asa trained junior lawyers the old-fashioned way, by involving us intimately in the work. He treated us as colleagues and solicited our input, and we observed at close range how he developed strategies and adapted them as circumstances shifted, thought through problems and their solutions, interacted with clients, prepared written materials, and conducted depositions and court hearings. When we prepared a draft brief or memo or letter for his review, he told us in direct terms what he thought of it and how it could be improved.

That training inspired me and, I suspect, nearly every associate who worked with Asa during his 30-odd years at the firm, to strive toward the multiple, and at times competing, standards that he set for himself, which included the following:

• Asa was fiercely competitive. A Korean War combat veteran, he often used military terms in talking about his cases. He wanted to win all the battles as well as the war.

• Asa kept the interest of the client paramount. He showed us that a settlement might best serve the client's interest, notwithstanding the wish of factions within a client to be vindicated and Asa's own hunger for outright victory.

• Asa toiled tirelessly to develop and refine the "right" argument, that is, the path or paths to winning that were analytically strong and supported by (or at least not inconsistent with) authority. He resisted arguments that sounded good but did not withstand close analysis or a careful reading of the cases.

• Asa was punctilious about being candid with judges. He spoke passionately about the importance of maintaining the firm's and his own credibility.

• Asa was mindful of, and at times perhaps fixated on, lawyers' inefficiency and its impact on costs. He wrote memos advocating more and better forms of institutional organization. Before files were retrievable through computer searches, he devised a decimal-based system for case files that others adopted. He claimed to have tried "every known organizational device" to put order to the files in his office.

• Asa saw himself, and his colleagues, as practicing a venerable and honorable profession. That perception was clearest, perhaps, when he labored over a brief or other submission to a court or a client. A student of rhetoric and a master of written expression, Asa pushed hard to arrive at the optimal organization and just the right words, excising those that were not needed to explain or persuade. The result was precision and clarity, embellished by an occasional aside or turn of phrase that provided an inimitable flair, that appeared to have come easily. Asa was an excellent editor with an eye (and a pen) for creeping obfuscation or prolixity.

I learned quickly not to try to imitate his unique style and, more slowly, to appreciate the self-discipline and hard work required to write succinctly and precisely.

Asa was able to practice at a level that met or surpassed all these standards, in part because of his remarkable intelligence, breadth of knowledge, and range of talents, and in part because he pursued the practice with unflagging energy and enthusiasm. To me, there were two elements that enabled Asa to push himself as hard as he did. First, he loved being a lawyer, or at least he appeared to, most of the time.

Asa seemed to enjoy almost every aspect of the practice: the intellectual challenges, the service of clients, the crafting of strategies and arguments, the interactions with his partners, with associates, with adversaries, and with colleagues in the Litigation Section. Some of that rubbed off on everyone who worked with him.

Second, Asa injected his wonderful sense of humor into almost everything he did. His colorful and witty memoranda have long been legendary at

Debevoise, and some of them will now reach a wider audience. But Asa used this gift in other ways. He could tell a joke or humorous story just when it was needed to break the tension at a meeting. In the pre-email age, when lawyers communicated with each other orally, his passing observations about the law or lawyers, politics, or the state of the world, or any of the arcane areas of science, history, or philosophy in which he was well read were laced with humor, often directed at himself. He clipped items from newspapers and magazines, scrawled marginal comments directed to particular lawyers, and left them on their chairs in the early morning. My favorites, for obvious reasons, are a series of salacious headlines and snippets from the *New York Post* reporting on the paternity suit against the actor Jack Klugman. Asa regularly sent me the *Post*'s descriptions of "Klugman's" activities with comments like: "I never knew what a swinger you were!" and "Have you no modesty, Klugman?" That was a terrific way to start a day.

I am pretty sure that I did not enjoy the practice of law as much as Asa did. And I know I'm not nearly as funny as he was, though it's not for lack of trying. But the enjoyment and appreciation for humor that Asa inspired helped me through many long days and late nights, and made me a happier, and I think a better, lawyer.*

Steven Klugman

* As an editor, Asa was death on footnotes. He typically removed them, often with the observation that a footnote reflected the author's indecision about whether to include the material. But lots of his memos have footnotes; my copy of the Guidelines has 17. I therefore feel entitled to a footnote about footnotes.

Steve Klugman was an associate and then a partner of Asa's at Debevoise and Plimpton LLP.

An Officer and a Gentleman

During the Korean War, an army sergeant said to his commanding officer on the last day of that officer's tour of duty, "We always felt safe with you, Lieutenant Rountree." Asa considered those words to be the highest praise he had ever received. In that early and definitive praise of Asa by one of his men, there is an enduring truth.

Asa was someone to be relied upon, a solid and thoughtful person with uncommonly sound judgment. He was never superficial or prone to impulsive reaction. Soon after we met many years ago, Asa talked to me about what he felt was the true role of a litigator. He explained his view that the litigator's role was not, in the first instance, to make a problem go away, minimize it, or otherwise render it manageable, because those objectives take time to attain. In Asa's view, his role as a litigator was, in the first instance, to make clients feel confident that they could leave their legal problems or concerns with him—to shift their problems from their shoulders to his—and go about their own business.

Clients, colleagues, and friends alike understood that his word was good, and they were certain they could rely upon him. If Asa's image were rendered in marble, a prospect that I am sure would horrify him, the only truly proper inscription would be: "We felt safe with you."

Apart from that Asa in marble, another Asa was constructed in humor. Our relationship was built, though not entirely, upon shared stories. He told me stories like that of his successful effort to suppress the pornographic film *Debbie Does Dallas*, on behalf of the owner of the Dallas Cowboys football team, who felt that the film put the team's cheerleaders, the Dallas Cowgirls, into a poor light. I asked Asa how many times he had seen the film, and he said with a smile he had seen it quite a few times in order, in his words, "to acquire a working knowledge of the evidence." (In truth, Asa was so appalled by pornography that, I believe, he never saw the film, but rather sent one or more associates, and the case turned upon intellectual property issues rather than upon the film's pornographic nature.)

Asa sent me pieces he had written (like those included in this book) in the guise of prospectuses "issued" by his alter ego, the "Magnus Gallery," which, as he said, had "the exclusive representation of his paintings." In turn, I sent him things I wrote, including three alternative versions of a letter of reference he requested from me in connection with his purchase of a cooperative apartment. I thought I would share those letters with you. I should note first that I was pleased when I learned that Asa had kept those letters for more than 20 years, but then, upon reflection, I knew Asa kept everything. In my covering letter for the three letters I wrote for Asa, I noted, "If you have trouble figuring out which one to submit, perhaps you should consult [your broker]."

The first of the letters contained only three lines addressed to the board of directors of the cooperative corporation:

> I know Asa Rountree. Asa Rountree is my friend. You're no Asa Rountrees, but don't let this stop you from letting him buy an apartment in your building.

The second letter, also tongue in cheek, is too long to reprint in full, but included the following passages:

You should count your lucky stars that I have the opportunity to warn you about this Asa Rountree character before you let him into the building. Have no doubt that admitting Asa to your premises will depress the value of your property below the level of the FDR Drive. . . . I am frankly surprised that you are even willing to entertain his application. Don't you know that Asa attempted to pass himself off as a famous painter, offers unregistered securities in his bogus art gallery and other phony ventures, attends pornographic movies, and goes to parties in various disguises? How are your doormen going to cope with the security problems posed by tenant-impersonators? . . . In the circumstances, the only reasonable course left to you is to approve his application. . . . The worst that could happen is that the old tenants will sue you for breach of fiduciary duty, and the new tenants will sue you for fraud. Don't get alarmed at this prospect; just hire Rountree. He is an expert on these matters, and I am sure he can extricate you from your problems.

The third letter, the actual reference, was as follows:

Asa Rountree has been my friend for many years. Asa is a true gentleman and warm companion, combines wisdom with a sense of humor, scholarly interests with sporting activities, and deeply held convictions with an openness and willingness to listen to others. You cannot overestimate the high regard I have for him. . . . You have the opportunity to have Asa Rountree as a neighbor. That opportunity should not be lost.

Each of these letters captures qualities of Asa that are best illustrated by his own words, many of which may be found in this collection.

Carl Robert Aron

Carl Robert Aron is an attorney and businessperson. He was a friend and colleague for more than 35 years and, from time to time, a client of Asa's as well.

The Pack Rat: A Fable

There once was a pack rat who lived in a tree
Where he collected much garbage with the greatest of glee.
He snickered and snorted, amassing his junk —
Till you wondered just why the tree hadn't sunk.
'Twas true, he didn't know all that he had,
So compulsive was he in his hurry to add
One more paper, one more book,
And on and on, till the branches shook.
There was just one thing he couldn't abide,
Which gave him wild thoughts about ratricide:
How could those ninnies ensconced in their holes
Exist in small burrows which held so few scrolls?
So he sent out a memo, that all would be sure
To know that their methods were poor, oh so poor.
"Come live in a tree, you'll have so much space.
So what if you never know what's in the place."
All of the pack rats heeded his words,
Forgetting that trees are for squirrels and birds.
They rushed to the maples, dogwood, and oaks,
Only to find the whole thing a hoax.
They fell to the ground, bang, with a thump,
Each thinking to himself, "Am I a big chump!"
For he was a special pack rat, you see,
He was the only one who could live in a tree.

Standish F. Medina Jr.

Standish F. Medina Jr. was Asa's colleague and law partner.

In Praise of Noisy Neighbors

While I never worked with Asa Rountree, in the sense of being assigned to one of his matters, I have learned as much from him about lawyering (said as a word of at least five syllables) as I have from anyone else in my career. Like many of my colleagues, I still consult a dogeared copy of the "Guidelines" reproduced in this book, which when used to its fullest is not just for new lawyers taking baby steps out of their offices; it is also a primer for being a good supervisor, editor, team leader, and instructor. Like *The Elements of Style*, Asa's guidelines should be read annually, forever.

I also had the joy of learning from Asa directly. Actually, I didn't have a choice. Asa Rountree was not a quiet man. He had a loud voice and a louder laugh. For several years when I was junior associate and he a senior partner, my small office was two doors down from his huge corner space. Asa had opinions and ideas, and to my great good fortune, he kept neither to himself.

Asa was no Luddite and, early on, bought his own photocopier, called RPOOXI, which sat next to his secretary's desk. Colleagues of all vintages would come to visit Asa and the copier, and my door jamb was often closer than his couch as a place to hold conversations about active matters, changes in strategy, pithy new sentences for upcoming briefs, recently read novels, tennis grudges, and politics of the day.

The sound levels in our corner reached the point that someone—perhaps the poor person between his office and mine—must have complained. Asa sent a memo entitled "Southwest Corner of 24th Floor" to the Debevoise office manager:

> In this neck of the swamp, we do not believe in the use of the intercom system. I shout at Maureen [Asa's secretary]. Maureen shouts at me. [Roger] Podesta shouts at Ivy. Ivy shouts back (although Ivy has a soft voice and is better behaved than the rest of us). Anne Cohen works a lot with Podesta. Podesta shouts at Cohen. Cohen shouts at Podesta (Cohen can really shout). RPOOXI itself makes a terrible racket. [Standish] Medina is always hanging around RPOOXI. He has a loud mouth, too.

Perhaps, Asa wrote, the answer was "to be sure that the firm is making full disclosure to potential occupants of 24SW."

It was noisy, but closing my door would have been both churlish and dumb. I was learning about the practice of law as a collaborative exercise, which in many ways is a primary takeaway of the writings gathered in this book. Asa taught me that, if we are lucky, we work with colleagues who are smart, curious, and imaginative and who will put their cases aside for an hour to help us hash out problems in ours. In an age of email, videoconferencing, and virtual workplaces, it helps to remember that, sometimes, you can do your best work by hollering down the hall.

Anne Cohen

Anne Cohen was a colleague of Asa's and became a partner at Debevoise & Plimpton LLP after Asa retired from the firm.

A Farewell to Asa

I think of Asa Rountree in stone-carved captions, such as those for Theodore Roosevelt on the arching entrance to the American Museum of Natural History ("Statesman—Historian—Naturalist . . . ."). In Asa's case:

Lawyer—a man who loves the law and lawyers, and the strengths, frailties, and rascalities of clients, opponents, and fellow barristers.

Bible quoter—"And Asa did that which was pleasing in the eyes of the Lord his God" (2 *Chron.* 14:2). I cite, of course, the King James Bible. That's the only one Asa quotes; he accepts no substitutes. A well-thumbed KJ (with concordance) was always close at hand in his office. We may have three rabbis and two priests at D&P, but I'm not sure how many quick-to-hand Bibles are in the office. The Biblical Asa, Solomon's great-grandson, walked in

God's ways. Not always, but often enough to stand out from a long list of kings who were idolaters, adulterers, and whorers after strange gods. Our Asa, too, walks—if not always—in the ways of the Lord.

Defender of his country—We've all seen on Asa's office wall a photograph of a younger, pistol-packing Asa, who may well have had hair under his bar-bearing helmet. Asa was an infantry officer in Korea. One day, patrolling a valley up north, he ordered his tired men to take a quick break in the bushes on the hillside. While his men sat, a North Korean patrol came down the valley, and Asa's unit shot it to pieces. Had the Korean patrol taken a break, and Asa's men kept going, it would have been the other way around. That kind of experience gives one pause and perspective, and helps one to understand the importance of the aleatory.

Stand-up speaker—Asa usually stands up to speak. As he puts it, "If I stand up, I get tired sooner and I won't speak too long. Shorter remarks are better remarks." It is a pleasure and an edification to hear Asa speak, for however long he likes to talk.

Painter—Here, words fail me. A picture is worth quite a few words, especially if the wordsmith (Magnus Gallery) is closely related to the painter (R. Brant).

Writer of memos—Memos that enlighten, probe, even startle. I'm old enough to remember the bombshell memo in which he announced that, after having been J. Asa Rountree all his life, he was dropping the "J," and henceforth would be simply Asa Rountree. I sent the memo back to him with a scribbled note: "Esus Christ, is nothing sacred?"

Tennis player—noted for determination and guile (I didn't say style).

Teller and hearer of jokes—few printable. What a pleasure to hear Asa's explosive laugh!

Teacher—Who among us has not learned from Asa? To name a single example, his "Guidelines for Work Being Done under My Supervision," is an incomparable guide to the litigator's world.

And one more caption:

Colleague and friend—whom we cherish, whose wisdom and warmth and humor in our midst will be deeply missed.

Meredith Brown

Meredith Brown was a colleague and partner of Asa's at Debevoise & Plimpton LLP. This essay was written on the occasion of Asa's retirement from the firm in 1991.